Whispers from the Shadows

Second Edition, Published 2014

Written by Steven Trustrum

This edition of Whispers from the Shadows is dedicated to my lovely wife, Erin, and amazing son, William. Without them, I'd still be in the dark.

www.misfit-studios.com

www.trustrum.com

Permission is granted to use these works for educational and review purposes, but none may be republished elsewhere, in whole or in part, beyond the confines of fair use without the author's express permission.

Woman's image on cover care of www.shutterstock.com.
All other works contained herein are Copyright 2014, Steven Trustrum.

ISBN 978-0-9879106-1-5

Author's Introduction

Someone is very likely to say that publishing one's own poetry oneself is the peak of arrogance, pretentiousness, and vanity, and they would likely be correct.

There is no easier way to be published than to do it oneself. However, seeing as how I have my own small press company, I'm allowing myself this small indulgence with no delusions regarding my ability as a poet.

Oddly, some of the poems contained within this work were viewed as good enough by others (I know ... crazy, crazy people) to otherwise be published. Some have been published in various independent magazines and news prints, school publications, and have even been taught within a few classrooms.

The poems herein span a number of years before I essentially stopped altogether as other, more lucrative (and mercenary) writing projects drew my attention in other directions with the rabid scent of dollars and fame (okay, at least I got paid. Sometimes) And yet, looking back on some of my poems, I realize nothing else I have written has made me as proud or given me as much joy (and sadness) as these works.

They are the undiluted thoughts, memories, and emotions I have rarely shared with anyone, even those closest to me. Unfortunately for you, the innocent reader, we poets are far more pompous when it comes to finally granting such things their freedom.

While I am confessing things, I should add that I catered to my vanity yet more by touching up and re-writing many of the works before adding them to this collection (and yet again for the second edition.) Some were first penned over a decade previous and, looking back on them now, I could not help but correct what I read while transcribing them.

While admitting that the process of polishing and touching-up was necessary, I have endeavored to leave the pulse and flavor of each poem untouched. Being so far removed from the event, emotion, or thought that inspired the work so many years later, I cannot now be certain I could remain faithful to the inspiration were I to alter it too much.

As I said: vanity.

No apologies, however, because we all have to stick to what we are good at.

> Steven Trustrum July 6, 2006
> (appended August 8, 2014)

Table of Contents

The Woods of Avalon	6	The Thespian	41
Birth of a Man	7	My Mask	42
Journey	9	Martyrs	43
Silence	10	Photographs	44
Corrosion	11	A Passive Discourse	45
The Face in the Night	12	Conflict	46
The Winds	13	Reflection	47
Dreamwalk	14	Epitome	48
Sunday Morning Ditty	15	My Resplendent Creation	49
The Bird of Happiness	16	The Not-So-Horror Story	50
What the Trees See	17	Baneful Sun	51
Seeds Don't Always Need Water	18	Night Blossom	52
A Vision of Night	19	Wind	53
The Arrogance of the Ignorant	20	King of Thieves	54
The Angels Cometh	21	Omnipotent	55
A Turn of the Heart	22	Chasing Dawn	56
Who Needs It?	23	Teardrops	57
The Heart of Denial	24	Covert	58
Comprehending Insanity	25	Seasons Change	59
The Raging Fear	26	Silent Morning	60
The Happy Clown	27	One Word Unspoken	61
The Schism	28	The Second Coming of Prometheus	62
Tribute to a Fool	29		
Penny	30	Effort	63
Snowfall	31	Beauty Concealed	64
A Few Corrections	32	Scars	65
First Kiss	33	Death of a Man	66
Where Hides the Genie?	34	The Bane	68
As I Remember …	35	Tomorrow's Bounty	69
Night Crawls In	36	Singing into Nothing	70
A Wall Too High	37	The Day the World Whispered	71
Rough Riders	38		
Orchestra	39	Whispers from the Shadows	72
Circle of Paradox	40		

The Woods of Avalon

Taste the cold upon your throat,
The steam escaping, as a spirit given to flight.
Smell the fragrant, all-encompassing pine,
Soaking through the senses with bitter joy.
I hear the woods call and restrain myself,
Wanting to run amongst the ageless giants of wood
Aside their green progeny.
Free of man's will and humanity's burden;
I walk amongst them, a part of their world,
Even if only briefly.
I am in awe of their ageless power,
As if asleep.
Sadly, I turn to go home,
Back through the watching giants.

Birth of a Man

I sit upon the precipice,
Awed by the beauty of honored twilight and
    golden waters.
Eyes gleam beneath the silver moons of
    sky and flesh.
Liken unto the sight of man,
Looking forever outward.

The waves resound against my cliff like a
    drum crying for war,
Answered only by the silence of my thoughts and
    the soft beating of nature's own heart.
Liken unto the hearing of man,
Listening forever outward.

The salted winds strike my nostrils,
    the sea's sweetness born upon its breath.
A feral aroma of untamed flowers and
    untrod fields causing my mind to sway.
Liken unto the snout of man,
Sniffing forever outward.

The gentle breeze plays across my face,
    caressing it like an old friend.
The Dawn has drawn its fingers across my naked being,
    keeping it from the cold clutches of darkness.
Liken unto the hand of man,
Grasping forever outward.

The waters speak to me and I
    answer their siren's call.
I live for the wonders of that voice,
    telling me my world's past, present and future.
Liken unto the lips of man,
Speaking forever outward.

Thus does my consciousness seek its eternal peace,
For no winds shall lift me there,
Nor carry me on to Utopia, for Eden did not want me.
So I shall strike outward,
    striving as I have done all through time.
Liken unto the thoughts of man,
Searching forever inward.

Journey

The endless sky of deepest blue,
Reaching into infinity with calming hands.
I think that I should like to go there,
Flying upon wings of thought,
Upon the winds of imagination.

My logic frees my creative soul,
Allowing it to swim amongst the ether and
Islands of virgin white.
I fly to be free and I cry for those
Whose feet will not allow them to leave the
Ground.

Silence

Strings of fallen thoughts and
    Sinking dreams,
My hopes crash against the walls of
    Realism.

I thought I could avoid it but
    The blackness has tracked me down,
Stalked me as the tiger
    Hunts the mouse.

Striving means very little to a
    World that is blinded,
Sticking pins in my eyes so that
    I may share of its bliss.

Place the coins upon my darkened orbs,
    Embalm me with the truth of my existence;
Wind me in the despair of my beliefs
    and Cry for the starving of my convictions.

Like a string of plastic baubles,
    We have lost our sparkle and are
Now just for show, a gaudy trinket.

Corrosion

The wind blows with fury

Striking the cliff like a fist

The rocks fall like tears

The Face in the Night

You stare at me from across the void,
    Your face hidden by shadow.
Only the whiteness of your eyes is revealed;
    Beacons against the black.

Why do you stare? Why do you follow?
    You crawl through my mind,
    An invader of my consciousness.

I can no longer drive you away,
    Your power is too great and my
    Will never knew strength.

I am yours.

The Winds

Nature's breath howls outside the glass,
    a voice of ordered chaos and
    determined fury.

Its power whips the leaves about,
    playing as a child does with
    its fragile toys.

People walk with resignation and fear,
    bent against the strength, trying to
stay that which is power and fluid.

But then I remember,
    a window without wind
    is merely transparent glass,
    staring outward forever upon a vacuum.

Dreamwalk

Screaming, feeling, fleeing, streaming,
Wherever I am, I'll be dreaming.
I think I may, I think I might,
Pray I don't have a dream this night.
Swing the sword, turn the clock,
Through my mind the Sandman walks;
Rushing forward, running fast,
Just how long will this nightmare last?
Stinging words, biting thought;
Against my mind I have fought.
All the while I've been weeping,
But, surprise, surprise, I've not been sleeping.

Sunday Morning Ditty

A million years,

A million beers,

The price for both is a million tears.

The Bird of Happiness

The bird in his hole would never have thought
The end of his life would come with the
Crack of a gunshot.

What the Trees See

These are the days of our demise;
October has come, leading winter by the hand.
Creeping its fingers across the dry earth,
Harsh cold pays its regards.

Gone are the days of renewing, swallowed,
Made extinct by the coming of frost.
Our children lay buried beneath the white,
Hidden from our view and left alone in the dark.

Forgotten are the days of growing,
Consumed, like Jonah, by the age of sleep.
Our roots are our lifeline, remains of past seasons and
Reminders of life under the warm sun.

These are the days of our extinction,
For they are the fields and forests of tomorrow,
The life and breath of the future.
Yet, knowing this, we have left them to be buried,
Alone, blanketed by the cold and the dark.
We have left them to the coming winter.
Our children, the seeds of beyond.

We have stolen their days of hope and become undone.

Seeds Don't Always Need Water

Lost in the infinite waters of dark anger
    are the drowning seeds of love and hope.
Each clings to the other in desperation,
    watching helplessly as the water presses
    them farther down, away from the shrinking light.
The sun reaches out to the receding seeds
    in a desperate attempt to save them
    from the embracing darkness.
Grey steam curls skyward as the black water
    quenches the fire of the sun's fingers,
    causing them to recoil in pain.
Defeated, the sun watches hope and love
    slowly drown, wanting to save them
    but unwilling to risk the pain.
Who will risk darkness of anger's waves?
Who shall bear the pain of that which
    extinguishes the sun's bright flame?
Shall you brave the waters?
Shall you risk extinction of your light?
Decide quickly for the seeds, sink down farther
    and soon they shall be out of reach.

A Vision of Night

Every eve a silver orb rises,
Readying the night for the coming of
    the stars.
In each blink of those distant suns,
    like sequins on velvet,
Is a narration of a million years past;
    an era long changed and evolved.
Heaven smiles down upon those who dare to
    look up and ponder
An infinite realm of cold and vacuum,
Dragged out between the planets
    and your upraised hands.
Watching eyes gaze upon you every night,
    blinking against the black,
Inviting you into their company,
    welcoming you amongst them in the sky;
Calling your name and asking you to reach higher,
    before the coming of Sol
Kills their vision … until the silver orb
    again walks the night.

The Arrogance of the Ignorant

I walk through the shadows with
    my eyes closed, for the
    darkness of my mind brings more
    comfort than the darkness of reality.

I walk through the lighted halls with
    my eyes closed, for the
    illumination in my thoughts is safer
    than the overwhelming brilliance of
    the world's corridors.

I close my eyes against all that
exists and pray for the birth of a wish.

The Angels Cometh

Here they come, singing songs of redemption,
Songs of sorrow, songs of dismay.
Their tune flows into my ears like
Tears through your fingers.
Their melody apologizes for the promises
Unfulfilled and for the vows yet taken.
However, their harmony brings a
Promise of its own, a vow of
Warmth and love, of joy and grace.
But I can see beneath their shawls of
Bone white, their fool's gold hair.
I can see their gaunt, colorless hands,
Their black molting wings, their red sunken eyes.
They are the horsemen, come to bear witness
To the end of my world.
I do not wish these riders of palest white
To sing my eulogy, nor inscribe my tombstone,
So I shall allow the world to continue.
Across the Earth I shall ride my radiant horse,
Its light keeping the shadows at bay,
Searching for a song that will fulfill the
Promises and make no apologies.

A Turn of the Heart

With a turn of the heart
    my world becomes a jumble.
I see you and my breath stills,
    stolen by the all-encompassing beauty behind your armor.

With a twist of the lip
    your smile draws me in.
Your words singing forth like angel's harping,
    a hidden whisper upon the winds.

With a glance of your eyes
    you lock me away,
    trapped within a cage of my own making.

Who Needs It?

What is shadow without light?

Grey without black or white?

All is darkness within a vacuum of despair.

The Heart of Denial

In the sea of your tears
I find myself drowning.
Under the light of your eyes
My body bursts into flame.
Within the cage of your heart
I am trapped and put on show.
No saw can cut these shackles,
No blade can tear my bonds.
Penitently, I bang my head against the bars,
    screaming for the sustenance long denied.
Yet you watch me starve, unwilling to offer up
    the love I need to survive.

Comprehending Insanity

Faster and faster it spins away,

Spiraling off into the fog of your conscious.

Quicker than perception, reality is

flying from the grasp of your control.

Like an animal in metal jaws,

Your eyes widen with fear at the prospect of the

Death of sanity and the loss of reason.

Poisoned flowers fill your vase,

Tainted by the corruption of your spirit.

A vortex of darkness and pain,

Howling forth your madness.

Grab my hand, quick, before

Oblivion swallows you whole.

The Raging Fear

All these years of fear and woe,

Reminding me of Old Man Poe.

The black, the shadows, the darkness deep,

Robbing me of my evening's sleep.

Bone white fog rolls forth like a chilling wave,

A guiding carpet to my waiting grave.

With fear I run, I flee, I cry,

Hoping against hope that I shall not die.

All this fear has got me wired,

But from the black speaks a voice:

"You can run, but you'll only die tired."

The Happy Clown

The Happy Clown cares not for fear,

He laughs and smiles with his good cheer.

He hides behind his smirk and grin,

But what will happen when the lights go dim?

He removes his make-up, his ghostly pallor,

His big red shoes, his squirting flower.

He is just a man like you or I,

He hurts, he feels, he frowns, he cries.

So when at the circus next time, if you see a clown,

Remember, upside down, that make-up smile is just a frown.

The Schism

Distance has no meaning to us for

We are a world of just you and I.

You are the earth and I am the sky,

Trapped around you for all eternity.

My kisses for you are as plentiful as the

Rain plunging into soil below.

We are separate and yet together;

Two halves of one whole.

A specter in my mind, you haunt me like a

Spirit of the ether, a symptom of love's madness.

You are a thief in the night, having slipped past my guard

And taken a piece of my heart.

I know that one day we shall be together,

But until then I am incomplete;

A shadow until the sky once more smiles down.

Tribute to a Fool

Oh, flush my heart

Gentle flower,

For here I sit,

Sad and dour.

Missing the auspicious sweetness

And gracious bliss

Of the long awaited

Gentleness of my desired kiss.

I long for your lips,

The pain as my heart breaks,

Oh, capricious wonders,

What fools of us love doth make.

Penny

It is said that one cannot

Put a price on love, but I can.

It is the penny.

The penny is but copper,

A trifle,

Nearly worthless and easily disregarded.

Not so when the penny is saved

And joined with more of its own.

It is now a part of a treasure,

A trove of worth

Which can amount to so much

More.

Snowfall

Snow on grass,

Turning color to blank,

Drained and cold,

Damned to white.

A Few Corrections

You call yourself a shadow,
    though you are bright.
You say that you are darkness,
    though, in truth, you are light.
You say you are noise,
    though I say you are song.
You say all these things,
    though you are wrong.

First Kiss

An awkward smile,
A trembling hand,
No-man's land between us.
Huddled with fear,
Desperate expectations and
Trepidation of the unknown.
Approaching,
Shaking,
Eyes searching for a place to look.
Lips brush and
Skin tingles.
Nervous, surprised, humorous;
All three felt and seen,
Memories forever burned.
A laugh cuts the tension,
Makes these calm.
Eyes pierce eyes,
Smiles widen and
Hands part.

Where Hides the Genie?

If I wish hard enough, can I fly?
Should I dream long enough,
    Will infinity be mine?
A dream with no purpose is a dream wasted
And a wasted dream is death.
Life is the wish of a dream,
Given form and granted being.
If I wish hard enough, can I fly?
For if I cannot attain the air,
Ungrant my wishes and cage my dreams.

As I Remember …

Framed by light, caught by time,

A moment frozen in thought, trapped by mind.

Fuzzy edges from marching age,

Reality clashes with fantasy, a foggy dream.

Loss of clarity as seconds tick by,

I need a new moment before old moments die.

Youth is eternal at the cost of you;

Can I make the sacrifice and see the new?

Night Crawls In

Oh, golden iris

Of night's omniscient eye,

Where clouded vision

Looks down upon my

Silver face.

I look upon you and

Wonder what is hidden

Within the veil of your blackness;

Day cannot reveal it for

The illumination of Sol peels back your fingers,

And with them

Removes the wall of ebony beauty

That made the unseen so enchanting.

What is it that draws me to mystery,

To Mother Night's breast?

Perhaps it is better to ask why

The dark of night is drawn to me?

Who can ever answer this question and

Should we even bother to try?

Perhaps we should just be content to

Continue looking upon each other questioningly,

Conspirators in our mutual silence and darkness.

A Wall Too High

A war of song,
Battles of joy,
Each smile of your lips a
Contradiction of pain and bliss.
For are your lips not in plain sight
Yet beyond the reach of mine?
Is your smile not shielded by beauty,
A bastion against my siege?
Alas, I have found my ladders too short
And my armies too weak and lacking to
Gain the treasure of your heart.

Rough Riders

The foe of circumstance,

The vindictiveness of fate,

We are naught but children of time.

Who are our parents?

Is it knowledge or is it chance?

Can we reign in the beast or is

it too wild to be broken?

If we dig in our spurs we risk

Being thrown.

If such is the case,

One must decide whether we shall move aside

Or if we shall climb back up and ride the

Beast to Hell and back.

Orchestra

Playing a chord of disharmony,
My heart plays a symphony of chaos,
A cacophony of rage and remorse.

My pain is a falsetto, a tremolo,
Shattering my crystal soul and
Grinding the fragments to powder.

The strings have all broken,
The horns have all rusted.
My music is now silent and the
Band all rotting,
Killed by a song that
Has played out.

Circle of Paradox

Is left right? Is up down?
All is perspective and nothing is concrete.
Fact is a mist that conceals and obscures,
Barely allowing us to see our own hands
Even when they are thrust before our eyes.
Truth is an abstract,
A matter of relation,
Perhaps even a lie.
Hearken these words I've penned,
For I have given them existence,
Made them material and
They are indisputable.

The Thespian

Reciting, memorizing, cycling;

Looking upon the hollow stage,

The actor cries out his lines

Upon blank ears.

Though the house is empty,

All eyes watch him.

A forgotten word unnoticed.

A trembling voice not reviled.

No applause from phantom hands.

Flat noise falling dead,

Dying from the shadows,

Having lived for the crowd.

All eyes watch him.

Blind.

Put out by reality.

Darkened by the stage.

My Mask

A ghost plays there,
In my mind's eye.
Dancing within the light of the
Night's suns.
Lightly tracing the dark
With fingers of cloud white.
Singing through the naked trees and
Laughing with the spinning wind.
Spectral lips playing Pan's Pipes,
Music for my imagination,
A symphony for your affection.
Filtering down like gossamer,
Shying from the touch and
Fleeing from the gaze of silence.
Why should the dawn conquer the dark?
Let it stay awhile and
Cover all with mystery.
Let it linger and
Convey your secrets lest the
Sun burn away my hope.

Martyrs

A cry, a gasp, a scream!
Darkness all around,
Above and below,
Behind and forward.
Forward.
Forward into the black.
Millions of voices screaming
"I am the One!"
Defying their end.
"I am the One! I am creation!"
A beginning.
A life born of a massacre;
Seeds sown by death.
Death carried on love's wings.

Photographs

I take my photos in color,

For that is how I remember,

Full of sparkle,

Boasting shades and tones

With joyous light.

I take no photos in Black and White

For then all I can see is the shadow;

The dark lines and the angry spaces.

My photos must be in color

For without them I cannot remember
 the life.

Without the shades, I cannot remember the smiles.

Without the light, I cannot remember why
 I take photos at all.

A Passive Discourse

Did I not impassioned play
Upon the gentleness of day?
I plot deep down,
My heart craftily employed
Against my verbose mind
Upon which it has gainfully toyed.

Singing the shepherd's cry,
My flock being all before mine eye.
Thoughts speed on
To merrier times,
Without guided course
And absent of gilded rhymes.

Under my thumb an angel I do keep,
Robbed of her glory, a damned sleep.

Conflict

Inspired to sing

By a bird's silence,

Flowing through lips

Like symphonic friends.

Convinced to dance

By a crippled satyr,

Nimble as a breeze

Unleashed upon the woods.

Reduced to death

By the life of all others.

Reflection

A reflection is illusionary,
Altering with a turn of the head,
A tilt of the eye.
It appears different to all,
The image determined by
Where one's feet are planted and
The degree of illumination.
In order to accept the
Reality of the reflection
One must first accept the illusion
Of that which casts it.

Epitome

You should not be here,

Thinking on these words,

Waiting for an illusion to unfold.

You are the meaning,

You are the characters and the plot.

You are the author.

Metaphor drips from your fingers

As simile follows you like a wake.

Time is your anecdote,

Just as dimension is your page.

You should not be here,

Awaiting my altruism in shadow,

Stalking my caged, pedagogical prose.

You are the author and I merely your reader.

My Resplendent Creation

A canvas, stark white and barren,

A brush, fine and clean of impurity.

Dash, spot, stroke, dab.

Hues and complexions appear,

Without form only to take shape,

Mingling and spreading their face

To create a bastard entity of

Motley cohesion.

Perfect!

A landscape of chaotic message,

Of dilettante amazement and

Anarchistic symbolism of empty reflection.

Shadings, vectors, contrasts, complementation.

The primary and the secondary,

Shape and vacuum.

A desultory order of thought and connotation.

Marvelous masterpiece, ho!

A brush clumped and stained by you and I.

A canvas, scarred by form yet still veiled and blank.

The Not-So-Horror Story

"Stay here 'til morn', my wakeful son,"
Exclaimed Greybeard, filled with fright,
"There's a red ring 'round the silvery moon
And it portends naught but ill this night."
"Fear not, my father, leave now must I,"
said young Iliac, a boast upon his lips,
"Beneath that silver face with fiery hair I shall ride,
Sharpened blades upon my hips."
So leave he did, through darkened glens
And blackened woods of shadows in the night.
Yet home Iliac returned and there he slept,
In a vista free from malice safe until light.
While short this tale may be,
Seemingly pointless and unclear,
It tells the story of one who accepts
That with courage there remains no sleeping fear.

Baneful Sun

A day is only as good as

Its first ray of light;

Staring down like an eye of peril.

Civilization without civility,

Born of the Sun,

Raised by the flame,

All ending on a pyre of ash.

Night Blossom

Remembering your face
A blessed kiss of beauty
Upon the night sky.

Wind

Wind is the strength that gives flight to nobility

Wind is the fire beneath a wild horse's hooves

Wind is the artist that shapes cold mountain faces

Wind is the brush that sweeps colors across twilight skies

Wind is the voice that carries your words back to me.

King of Thieves

Can you see my heart, Raven,
Sitting there on your branch
As you stare at me?
Your call filters through to me,
Summons my attention, beckons my purpose,
So that I will capture this day for you,
A noble bird of carrion,
Of rotting flesh and castoff moments.
Wearing the crown of green leaves and a
    Cloak of a setting sun,
All framed, picture perfect,
Through my open window.

Omnipotent

A fallen god bends his knee

Before one of His tarnished houses,

Its arches having tumbled from heaven,

The civilized pulpit rotting back into the earth.

A trickle of tears from broken, glass eyes

Flowing through tiled riverbeds with cracked faces,

Anointing pagan spirits and totems.

Carpets of birthing green and decaying browns

Have eaten those of blood red and royal burgundies.

Roots of ancient parishioners slowly raise themselves

Upwards towards distant, deific lands,

Their slow journey pushing through the buttresses of antiquity,

Crying unseen in Time's shadow,

The prostrate god bows His head in submission.

Chasing Dawn

Pursuing the horizon,

That fleeing light,

Which struggles against the

Harsh blackness that

Peers over my shoulder.

I dare not turn around

For fear of being swallowed

Within the ravenous talons

Of impenetrable night.

Instead, I shall stare

Ever onwards towards the moon,

Existing with peril in twilight,

Forever Chasing Dawn.

Teardrops

A single tear hanging eternally,

Never falling,

Suspended like a crystal of prophecy,

Like a promised river,

A deluge of tentative expectation,

It harries a memory of

Bitter frailty or Scalding bliss;

None may tell until it has

Run its fated course and

That is an eternity away.

Covert

A racing beat,

Thriving on the memory

Of a cherished touch,

Warm with invitation and

Blessed by its glorious relation,

Pulsing on its way,

Boiling with fevered trepidation

Over the recall of faint breath and

Lips of ageless silk,

My blood challenges honored judgment.

I can hear the singing of my spirit

As it cries out for yours,

A desire for a joining of hearts,

An alliance of old souls,

A harmonious duet whose music

Was composed in star-written destiny.

Let the body not betray the intention,

An unknowing traitor

Of brittle masks,

Not capable of concealing that which shall not be returned.

Seasons Change

Why question the heart

When you know the mind;

The rationale of a

Forgotten season,

A whim gone dead and

Long burned away

By the newly encroaching summer?

Silent Morning

Let it sleep Let it be quiet

For day shall hearken

A noise of light and music

To shake the very dead.

One Word Unspoken

Holding the breath of strength

As the candle weeps thick time,

You contain your will even as

The lungs in your breast

Reach to burst with the fire

Of the unspoken word

That has become waylaid

Between heart and lips.

The Second Coming of Prometheus

How brightly burned the Inferno

Through the deep Black, Feeding upon the Darkness

Until it erupted forth,

A battling birth of a child

That was sired long before.

How expansive the Black,

Inhaling Inferno's rage,

Funneling it into the wound,

Shaping it into a form

Once known but thought forgotten.

Once forgotten but never forgiven.

Effort

Where rises the tide

Against a shore of malice?

Cliffs looming upwards towards perdition,

Watching from on high as

Hope crests and succumbs with finality.

Beauty Concealed

Those who believe the
    fog only conceals beauty
Have not yet learned to
    see the beauty of the veil itself.

Scars

How does the blind man know
When he's been abandoned
Within a white room,
Left alone with no
Windows or doors to the colors beyond?

How does the deaf man,
Strolling through the wild forest,
Know when all the birds have
Flown far away,
Soaring off into infinite silence,
Leaving no wings to flutter at his passing?

How does the mute man
Scream forth his rage and sorrow
When he awakens to his life
To find he envies those who
Are isolated from the sights and sounds
Of a world that is blind and deaf to his
Vacant words?

Death of a Man

I stand upon the precipice,
Charmed by the comfort of blessed morning and
    silver sands.
My eyes swell beneath the gilded Sun of
    earth and fire.
Liken unto the eyes of man,
Staring forever inwards.

The tempest blows the dust about like a
    horn sounding a dirge,
Mourned only by the silence of my tears and
    the harsh stilling of my ensorcelled heart.
Liken unto the hearing of man,
Hearkening forever inwards.

A parched presence haunts my nostrils,
    the barren's judgment carried by its howl.
The heralding odor of decaying petals and
    spent oases spin my thoughts into a tumble.
Liken unto the snout of man,
Sniffing forever inwards.

The harsh rain drives into my face,
    lashing out like a punitive foe.
The Moon has laid its palms across my naked being,
    pushing it away from the peaceful warmth.
Liken unto the hand of man,
Clinging forever inwards.

The sands speak for me, and I
    must heed their fated passing.
I fear the mysteries of that chapter,
Telling me my world's future and nothing more.
Liken unto the lips of man,
Whispering forever inwards.

Thus does my memory seek its eternal peace,
For no hope shall carry me there,
Nor remind me where I had discovered Utopia.
So I shall do it myself,
    fighting as I have done until death.
Liken unto the heart of man,
Struggling forever outwards.

The Bane

Let it slumber

Deep underground,

Rumbling,

Rolling,

Horror found.

Leave it to sleep

In twisting dreams,

Wistful,

Winsome,

Foreboding teems.

Let it not awaken,

And arise tonight.

Vindictive,

Vengeful,

Heavens alight.

Tomorrow's Bounty

How may the fallow field bloom

From seeds held in darkness

By a sun that shall never crest

The clouds borne on unwholesome

Winds of a failed night's wanting?

Singing into Nothing

And so does ragged breath

Sing a swallowed tune

Where the ground carries no bass

    and

The stars offer no guidance;

    twisting in an orgy of replete void.

The Day the World Whispered

Where do the fires stop,
If not in the heart,
As ashes rise high
O'er Bethlehem's rooftops?

When shall fear tremble,
If not with the heart,
Beneath pluming pillars
Streaming, grey, towards heaven?

Why should footsteps falter,
If not for the heart,
Where heavy shrouds fall
Upon the quiet depths of courage?

The world has become nearly silent,
Especially in the heart,
From hall to throne,
As a single whisper is shared,
Its echo lighting ever on.

Whispers from the Shadows

There's a voice I hear

When I stare into the dark,

Looking within, between and around the light.

Straining to listen,

Like a solitary candle struggles against Midnight,

I wait for the voice to awaken

So I no longer need suffer

Whispers from the shadows.

www.ingramcontent.com/pod-product-compliance
Lightning Source LLC
Chambersburg PA
CBHW071746040426
42446CB00012B/2486